Wheels

VENICE SHONE

ORCHARD BOOKS

baby wheels

pram

play wheels

roller skates

tricycle

skateboard

3

bicycle wheels

bicycle

St Raphael
GiTANE
CAMPAGNOLO

4

motorbike wheels

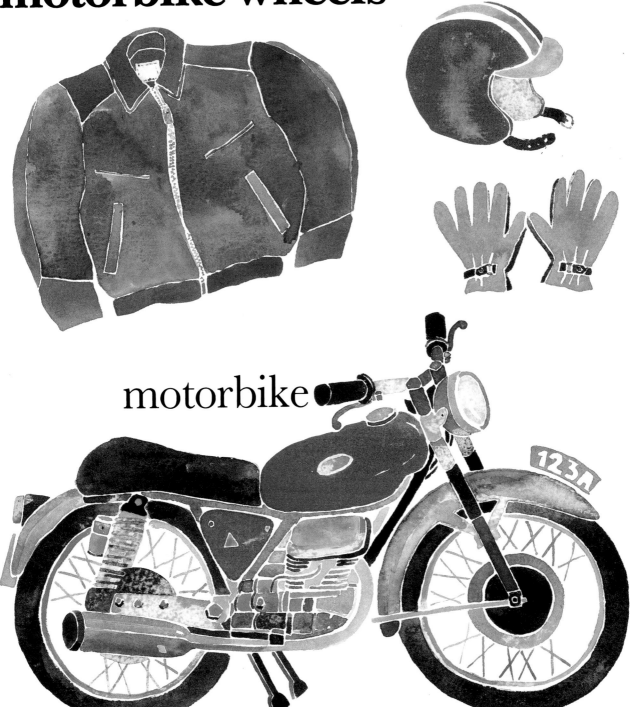

motorbike

5

6

racing wheels

racing car

car wheels

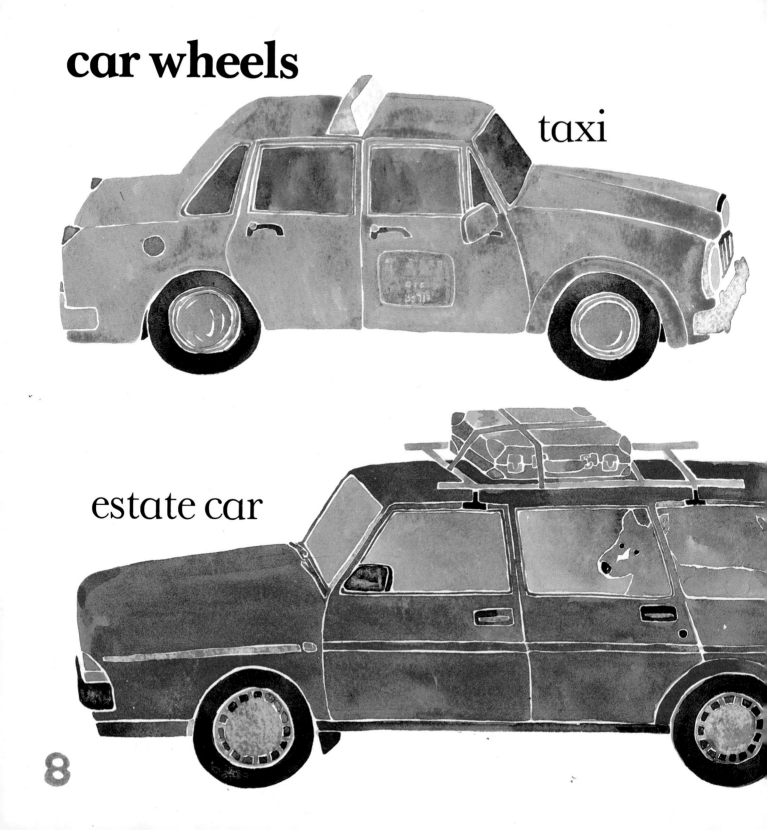

taxi

estate car

8

wedding car

learner-driver car

DRIVING SCHOOL

9

wheels on the bus

school bus

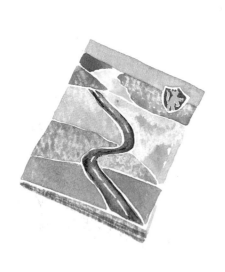

10

Bus

coach

11

baker's van

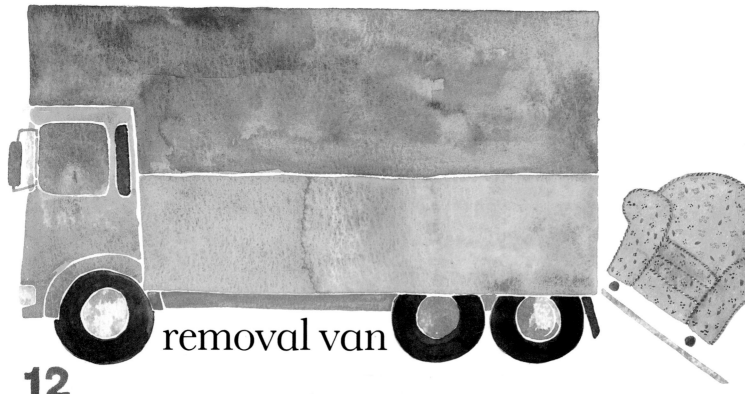

removal van

laundry van

florist's van

13

police car

ambulance

14

emergency wheels

fire engine

15

dump truck

wheelbarrow

16

working wheels

cement mixer

away-day wheels

22

luggage
trolley

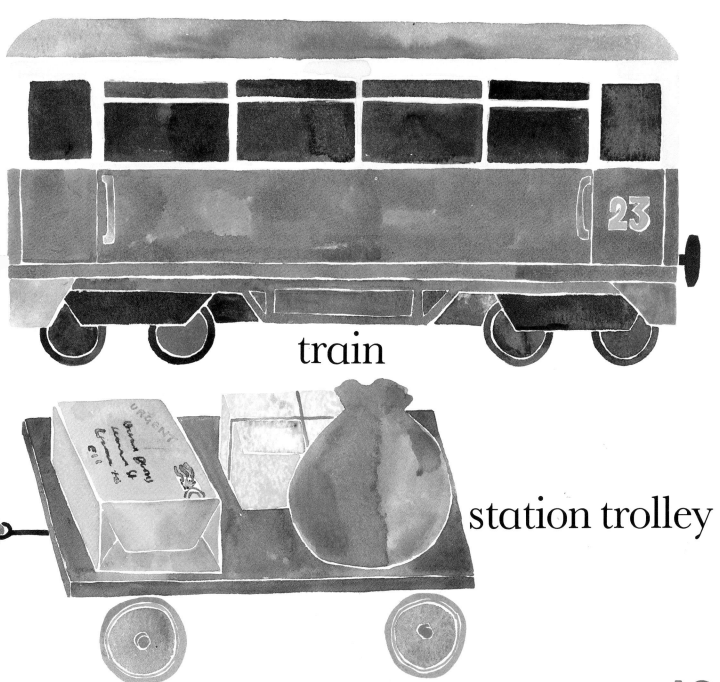

train

station trolley

19

up, up and away wheels

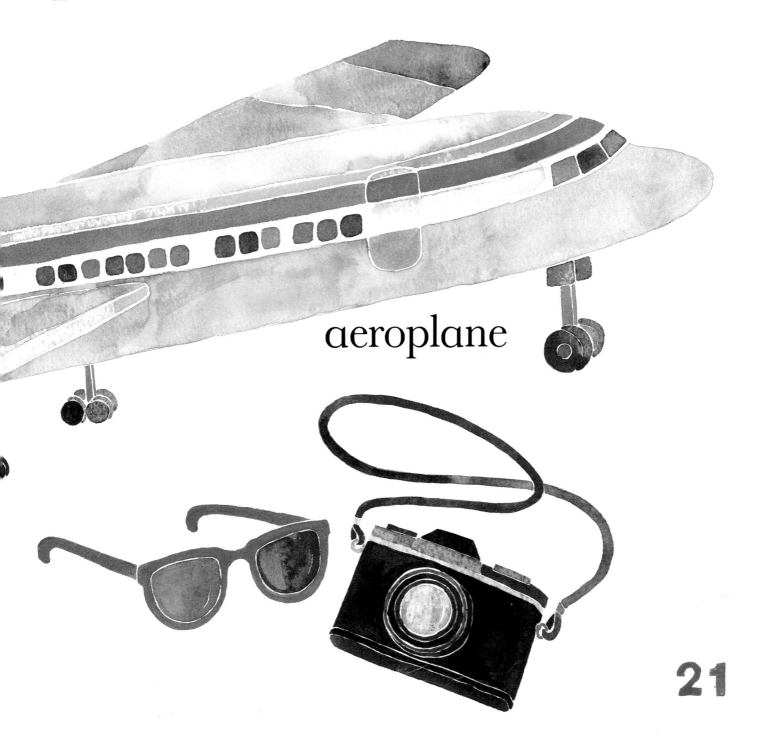

aeroplane

holiday wheels

jeep

boat

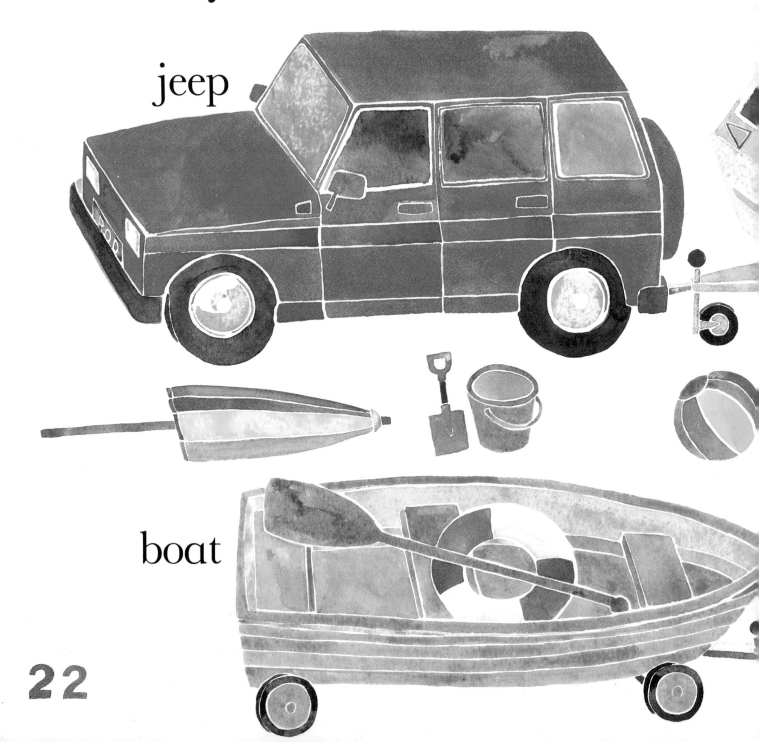

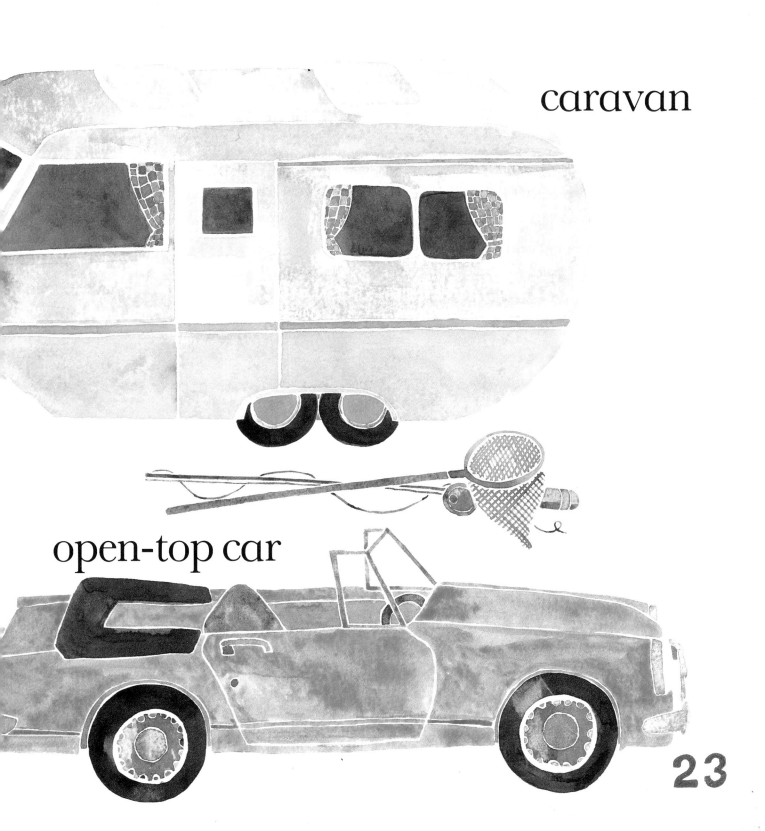

caravan

open-top car

23

wheels on wheels

car transporter

PRINTED IN BELGIUM BY
proost
INTERNATIONAL BOOK PRODUCTION